Stones, Walls and Watchmen

Deslee Campbell

Published by Deslee Campbell, 2024.

STONES, WALLS AND WATCHMEN

First edition. May 26, 2024.

Copyright © 2024 Deslee Campbell.

ISBN: 979-8224327935

Written by Deslee Campbell.

Table of Contents

Chapter 1
City of Gold

Jerusalem, the City of Gold, the heart and soul of the Jewish people, is like no other

city on earth. She is unique, yet she is like every city: dynamic, creative, crowded,

cosmopolitan. She is like a crown set in the Judean Hills, a queen of cities, yet her

enveloping and timeless embrace, the embrace of a mother, has been recognised sine

ancient times.

"Rejoice with Jerusalem and be glad for her, all you who love her ... for you will

nurse and be satisfied at her comforting breasts; you will drink deeply and delight in

her overflowing abundance." (Is. 66:10-11)

Yet Isaiah, the same prophet who spoke these words, perceived the child within her

soul: "You (Zion) will drink the milk of nations and be nursed at royal breasts." (Is.

60:16)

Jerusalem is eternal: the past, the present and the future reside gently together within

her bounds. She is as ancient as civilization, yet she has a youthful and vibrant spirit.

She is the mother of all cities, yet she is still a child. She is as mysterious as Lhasa, as appealing as Stratford-on-Avon, and as dynamic as San Francisco. For

architecture she rivals Brasilia, for history she surpasses even London and for

spiritual significance she has no peer on earth; neither Rome, nor Kyoto, nor

Banaras, nor Canterbury. As a place of pilgrimage for many nations even Mecca

itself is not her equal. Jerusalem is unforgettable, her impact is indelible. No one

visiting her, leaves untouched.

"If I forget you, O Jerusalem, may my right hand forget its skill... If I do not consider

Jerusalem my highest joy." (Ps. 137:5-6)

Yet four thousand years ago Jerusalem was not a Jewish city but a Jebusite city

called Jebus. This was at about the time Melchizedek was a ruler in the area.

Melchizedek, whose name means 'King of Righteousness', received tithes from

Abraham. He was the ruler of a city called 'Salem', which means 'Peace'; possibly

Jeru-Salem herself.

Plate 1.2. Orphel-David's City below Herod's Temple.
Model of the 1st century city. Photo: D. Campbell, 1988.

For the Jewish
people the saga of the city began when, on the advice of the
prophet Gad, David

went up and purchased a threshing floor on Mt Moriah from Araunah (or Oman) the

Jebusite (II Sam. 24:18ff). David built there an altar of the Lord and later set the

place aside for the construction

of the first permanent Temple of the Lord, which Solomon, his son, would build (II

Chron. 3:1).

Today this city, which David called 'Mt Zion' has been described as 'the heart and

soul of Israel'. In Scripture the word 'Zion' is used in various ways. It can mean not

only a particular hill in the Land, but the capital city, the whole country, or the people

themselves. Jerusalem is the capital of Israel, a city of just one million people. It has

celebrated three thousand years as the spiritual heart of world Jewry. This is why, in

1996, Jerusalem's Mayor, Teddy Kollek, invited all those who are named David to

go up to the city, to commemorate this tri-millennial anniversary.

Later David set aside the threshing floor for the construction of the first

permanent Temple to the Lord, which his son Solomon built. By far the most

significant thing about Zion, or Jerusalem, is that it has a special place in the

affections of the Lord God and in His plans for the future of mankind. Here the

Messiah chose to spend his last days and to die: here he rose from death and here he

will establish his kingdom. It is here, as the Scriptures proclaim, that the Holy One

has chosen to set His Name.

"May your eyes be open towards this temple night and day, this place of which you

said, 'My name shall be there,' so that you will hear the prayer... the supplication

of your people Israel...." (1 Kings 8:29)

Since David conquered it and established his capital there, Jerusalem's chequered

history has flowed with the blood of her citizens many times. How many times she

has been conquered? An indication can be obtained from this table, which shows

just some of the major events of Jerusalem's turbulent and bloodstained history:

DATE EVENT
B.C./B.C.E.
997 David conquered Jebus
922 Solomon built the First Temple
587 Nebuchadnezzar razed the Temple
538 Exiles returned from Babylon
520 Zerubbabel built the Second Temple
446 Nehemiah rebuilds the walls
333 Alexander the Great conquered the land
168 Antiochus Epiphanes desecrated the Temple
165 Maccabees Victory in the Jewish Rebellion
164 The Temple was cleansed & rededicated
63 Pompey's army took city

37 Herod, a Roman puppet, fought for his kingdom
22 Herod began to recreate or build the Temple

Jesus' birth

A.D./C.E.
64 Caligula's image to be put in Temple
68 Roman army invaded
70 Rome destroyed Jerusalem and the Temple
132 Bar-Kokhba's revolt against Rome
134 Hadrian's army defeated the Jews
135 Hadrian's Colonia Aelia Capitolina built on the site
324 The Byzantines ruled her from Constantinople
614 Persian rule, churches destroyed
640 Mohammedan Arabs took the City
691 The Dome of the Rock built
969 Conquest by the Seljuk Turks
1099 The First Crusade conquered the City
1187 Saladin defeated the Crusaders
1200 Egyptian Mamelukes took the City
1517 Ottoman Turks (Selim) took the City
1520 Suleiman the Magnificent reigns
1537 Suleiman rebuilt the City walls
1917 British took City in World War I

1947 U.N. vote for a Jewish Homeland
1948 Nation of Israel proclaimed as Arabs invade
1956 The Suez Canal Crisis
1967 The Six-Day War
1973 The Yom Kippur War
1982 War in Lebanon
1987 The First Intifada (Palestinian uprising) (1987-1993)
1991 The Gulf War - Iraqi Scud Missile attacks (1991-1993)
1996 Grapes of Wrath War in Lebanon (17 days)
2000 The Second Intifada (2000-2005)

This strife-torn chronology serves to show how important Jerusalem's defences have
  been throughout Israel's history. Though they were often futile, on occasions they
  held fast so that the City had to be starved into submission through a protracted siege.

Today her security is just as important as in ancient times as Jerusalem is
  simultaneously the capital and seat of the Knesset (the Israeli Parliament), the
  religious centre of Judaism, and the emotional heartland of World Jewry. Today
  Israel's defence system takes on a different appearance: tanks, 'planes and Patriots
  have replaced horses, battering rams and stone walls, but the spiritual lessons
  illustrated by her ancient defences remain, as does her God-ordained spiritual
  significance.

Chapter 2

Stones

Stones are extremely plentiful in Israel. During the Intifadas, Israelis were kept

constantly aware of this fact by Palestinian children whose strength and aim

damaged people, as well as the windows of cars and buses.

Stone has always played a major role in Israel's everyday life, whether it be for

millstones, for olive presses, for pavements, for walls and for buildings. A

regulation, first instituted by the British, requires that all buildings, if not built fully

of stone, at least must be faced with Jerusalem limestone. It is this beautiful stone

which gives the city its harmonious appearance and its golden glow in the setting

sun.

Virgin stones, uncut, were always required for any altar built unto the Lord from the

time when Noah built the first recorded altar of offering (see Gen 8:20).

"If you make an altar of stones for me, do not build it with dressed stones, for you

will defile it if you use a tool on it." (Ex. 20:25).

When bringing the people back from Egypt, Joshua marked both the occasion and the place of the crossing of the Jordan River by building an altar there, at Gilgal.

Twelve large stones were taken up from the riverbed, one carried on the shoulder of

a representative of each of the tribes. Thus the first altar to be built in the Land was

made of twelve large river stones.

A nine metre by seven metre altar of uncut stone has been discovered at Mount Ebal

near Shechem. This is believed to be another altar constructed by Joshua, one which

Moses had previously commanded Joshua to build on Mt. Ebal on the day when the

covenant was proclaimed and confirmed in the Land.

"When you have crossed the Jordan, set up these stones on Mt. Ebal, as I command

you today, and coat them with plaster. Build there an altar to the Lord your God, an

altar of stones." (Deut. 27:4)

The last Altar of Sacrifice to be constructed in Israel was made for the cleansing and

rededication of the Second Temple in 164 B.C.E., two centuries before the final

destruction of the Temple. The previous altar stones had been desecrated by the

Syrian despot Antiochus Epiphanes IV who sacrificed a pig on the altar and

dedicated the Temple to Zeus. The desecrated stones were laid aside in the Temple area - until the Messiah should come and explain what should be done with them.

But meanwhile Jewish outrage motivated widespread support for the revolt led by

the Maccabee family: Mattathias and his five sons especially Judah, Jonathan and

Simon. Israel threw off the Syrian yolk and restored Jewish independence, which

Plate 2.1. Stones on Jewish Graves, Mt of Olives. Photo: Ian Finnin, 2018.

lasted for one hundred and one years. The Festival of Hanukkah, which Jesus

attended, and which is called "the Feast of the

Dedication" in the New Testament (Jn. 10:22), commemorates this event. It is also

called the Festival of Lights.

Stone was also used for more sacred purposes: for example a stone is placed on a

grave to indicate that it has been visited. Two tablets of stone were, for many years,

among Israel's most treasured possessions. These were the stones upon which the

Ten Commandments were inscribed, and which were carried inside the Arc of the

Covenant from Mt. Sinai wherever the people went in the desert.

Stone

utensils were used in Temple ritual and in wealthy households, because, according

to Kosher Law, they are classed as impervious and therefore did not became

contaminated. By contrast, pottery pieces used by the poor, could become

contaminated, in which case they had to be broken. Despite their expense, priests

used stone household utensils in order to minimise the risk of impurity. Many such

vessels were discovered in the House of Noble Dimensions under the Jewish Quarter of the Old City, an area of the Upper City of Herod's Jerusalem in which the wealthy

lived. This particular house, owned by a priestly family, was destroyed when the

Romans burnt the Temple and the city in 70 A.D.

Tombs were natural caves or were hewn from large rocks after which a huge boulder

or a rolling-stone or a square stone was used to seal each one. In the 1st century,

Romans carved stones into sarcophagi but Jews carved them into ossuaries (bone

boxes) because they practised secondary burial so that their tombs could be

DESLEE CAMPBELL

Plate 2.2. Damaged ossuaries in an ancient necropolis on the Mt of Olives. Photo: Ian Finnin, 2018.

frequently reused. Ossuaries are generally considered to predate the destruction of

Jerusalem in 70 C.E. although the practice continued in remote locations for longer.

There are many 1st century and Herodion period repositories for ossuaries outside

of the city walls, including on Olivet, Mt Scopus and at Talpiot. In the 1930's an

inscribed ossuary was found in a cave on Mt Scopus. When translated it read,

"Nicanor and Alexa of Alexandria, the sons of Nicanor who made the doors." The

6th century Talmud maintained the tradition that Nicanor, an Alexandrian Jew,

brought splendid metal doors from Egypt for the Temple (t.Yoma 38a). Another

ossuary, discovered in the 1970's, is translated as, *"Simon the Builder of the*

Temple."

These people apparently proudly participated in Herod's construction work on

Temple Mount. [Dan Bahat, 'Second Temple in Jerusalem', in Charlesworth, Jesus

and Temple (Fortress, 2014), 72].

Stone is an indispensable material in maintaining Jerusalem's beauty today, and has

fulfilled many vital functions in the past, not least of which is the construction of the

city walls. The stones that now surround Jerusalem have seen the ebb and flow of the fortunes of many empires and much suffering for the Jewish people over many

centuries: yet, despite its tempestuous past, Jerusalem will eventually reach a period

of quietness, of true "Shalom".

"Jerusalem shall be raised up, and remain in its place... It will be inhabited; never

again will it be destroyed. Jerusalem will be secure." (Zech. 14:10-11)

When speaking about a future time in which compassion will be shown to Zion the

Psalmist compared compassion for her with caring about her stones. That is to say -

those who love her will demonstrate this by their caring attitude to, of all things, her

stones and her dust!!

"You will arise and have compassion on Zion, for it is time to show favour to her;

the appointed time has come. For her stones are dear to your servants; her very dust

moves them to pity." (Ps. 102: 13-14)

Does this affection for her dust and stones mean her ecology, her building stones and

her rebuilding program, or her archaeological remains and historic monuments?

Perhaps much more than just these. Many think that the thirst for the discovery of

their history, which makes archaeology a national pastime and a passion with Israel's

scholars, fulfils these prophetic words, as hundreds sift through the dust of the Land

during the warmer months.

The returning Ethiopian Jews, who have recently came back to the Land in two

waves, in 1984-5 and 1992, and who are still being regathered, poignantly

demonstrate that the Lord intended far more than secular and scholarly interest when

He inspired these words. The Ethiopian immigrants, like many of the olim who

returned to Israel in the 1950's, actually embrace the Land, and kiss the soil of their

new homeland. Pope John Paul's traditional kiss of greeting that was so widely

featured on television, was merely perfunctory compared with the joyous embrace

of Diaspora Jews when re-united with their Promised Land.

If one were to accompany some of the new immigrants from their first moments of

encounter with Eretz Yisrael, into Old Jerusalem, to their first glimpse of the

Western Wall, the Holy Kotel, a new understanding of the meaning of "her stones

are dear to your servants" could be reached. The Western Wall is no longer a wall

for wailing, but is certainly still one for tears.

Serious psychological trauma was experienced by many of those Ethiopians who

returned in 1984, in the wave of immigration called "Operation Moses", when they

discovered that there was no longer a Temple in Jerusalem. For thousands of years

they had lived by the Torah, the five books of Moses, in the earnest expectation that,

should they ever journey to Israel, all would be just as it is written. Thus many suffered severe grief, exacerbated by culture shock and homesickness for loved ones

they had been forced to leave behind in Ethiopia. They expected to find a glorious

Temple and found only a wall of stone.

It is before the stones of the Western Wall, the last vestiges of the glory of the

Temple, which Herod had restored during his reign (37 B.C.E. to 4 B.C.E.), that the

most heartfelt prayers are uttered and the most heart-rending tears are shed. It has

always been so. Rabbis and children, soldiers and notables have cried at this wall. In

1967 Prime Minister Golda Meir's tears mingled with those of the young soldiers

Plate 2.3. The Western Wall: men's section. Photo: Ian Finnin, 2018.

who recaptured the Old City. During World War II an Australian soldier sent a

snapshot home, on the back of which he had written, "Jews come here to pray. They

cry

tears on these stones. Even men do this !!" Indeed her stones have been dear to them

for centuries.

Another series of stones from the Herodion period may have been intimately

connected with Jesus' experiences in Jerusalem, and are not far from Temple Mount:

it is a pavement of Jerusalem stone. The Antonia Fortress is possibly the Praetorium

of Mark 15:16 and it was just north of Temple Mount. This massive complex was

much larger than the Temple itself. It was connected by two stairways to the Temple

colonnade known as Solomon's Porch, the area in which the first disciples frequently

met (see Acts 5:12).

This stone pavement, called the Lithostratos, now lies in the crypt below the convent

of the Sisters of Zion. Etched in its soft stone are some board-type games which

Roman soldiers played, to while away the time. One in particular is chilling -

illustrating the ancient's disregard for human life. Called `the game of a king' the loser lost his life, or a slave was put to death in his stead. On the stone pavement

called in Hebrew "Gabbatha", Jesus, in his last hours, was tried by the Roman

Governor, Pilate. Here Pilate publicly washed his hands before a large crowd (Mat.

27:24). Pilate ordered his execution there and many believe that this pavement is the

very spot.

"Then the Jews led Jesus from Caiaphas to the palace of the Roman Governor. By
now it was early morning, and to avoid ceremonial uncleanness the Jews did not
enter the palace they wanted to be able to eat the Passover. So Pilate came out.... he
brought Jesus out and sat down on the judge's seat at a place known as The Stone
Pavement (which in Aramaic is Gabbatha). It was the day of the Preparation of the
Passover Week, about the sixth hour" (Jn. 18:28 & 19:13-14).

From this pavement Jesus was taken, having been scourged, to be crucified.

"He was taken from prison and from judgement; and who shall declare his
generation? for he was cut off, out of the land of the living; for the transgression of
my people was he stricken" (Is. 53:8 A.V.).

The enemies of Israel have often attacked not only the people, but, strangely enough, also her trees and her stones. Titus, the general who later became Emperor of Rome, cut down all the trees in the vicinity of Jerusalem, as well as ordering the city's demolition - permitting only the retaining walls of the Temple platform and part of the Citadel to remain, as a memorials to the might of Rome.

During the Ottoman Period the Turks taxed Palestine's trees out of existence,

reducing the once beautiful land to a desert, and, more recently, arsonists have

deliberately burnt 20% of Israel's forests during the two Intifadas (the Palestinian

uprisings of the period 1987 to 2005). Sadly, arsonists also burnt the wild animals

of the Biblical Nature Reserve on Mt Carmel.

In these matters Israel's enemies have acted totally contrary to God's express plans

for the Land:

"`For I know the plans I have for you,' declare the Lord, `plans to prosper you and

not to harm you, plans to give you a hope and a future.'" (Jer. 29:11).

Chapter 3

Inscribed Stones that Testify to History

Inscriptions in stone left by the ancients require interpretation and rarely tell us

everything we want to know about the subject in questiion but they last well and

finding them is a delight. The most famous inscription found in Jerusalem may

well be the inscription inside Hezekiah's Tunnel, the original of which was taken

to Constantinople (Istanbul) during the Ottoman Period. It has been replaced by a

copy.

1) Hezekiah's Tunnel Inscription

This Hebrew inscription was found in 1880 but was created c.701 B.C. It bears the

name of King Hezekiah of Judah and was found 20 feet (6m) inside the tunnel

(from the Upper Pool of Siloam's entry point). King Hezekiah of Judah (716/15-

687/86) blocked off the water to withhold it from the Assyrians in anticipation of a

siege by King Sennacherib of Assyria (II Chron 32:3-30) and dug the tunnel to

bring the water of the Gihon Spring within the city walls (II Chron. 32:30).

Jerusalem was indeed besieged in c.701 BC but Hezekiah and the people, aided by

the prophet Isaiah, held on in faith (Is. 36:1-37:38). The Jewish historian Josephus

states that the Assyrian army succumbed to a plague-like disease (Ant. 10.1.5. (21).

Perhaps that was the case, because they withdrew without fighting, as was foretold

in II Kings 19:34:

"This is what the Lord Almighty says concerning the king of Assyria: He will not

enter this city or shoot an arrow here. He will not come before it with shield or

build a siege rampart against it. By the way that he came he will return, he will not

enter this city, declares the Lord. I will defend this city and save it for my sake and

for the sake of David my servant."

The tunnel is 533m long (1800 or 1749 ft) and was an engineering marvel in that

two sets of workmen with hand-drills dug from either end and met in the middle.

The inscription concludes: "on the day of tunneling each stone-cutter was striking

hard to meet his co-worker, pick after pick and the water began to flow."

Hezekiah's achievement is supported by II Kings 20:20f which adds: *"As for the*

other events of Hezekiah's reign, all of his achievements and how he made the pool and the tunnel by which he brought water into the city, are they not written in the

book of the annals of the kings of Judah? Hezekiah rested with his fathers."

2) The Theodotus Inscription

The New Testament indicates that, by the 1st century of the Common Era, the

synagogue was an established, semi-formalised institution in Galilee, although as

Plate 3.1. The Theodotus Inscription in the Israel Museum, Jerusalem. Photo: Ian Finnin, 2018.

recently as the 1960s it was believed that this did not apply in Judea or anywhere

within easy access to the

Temple and/or that synagogues were not designated buildings but simply meeting-

places, like house-churches.

The first evidence to challenge these opinions was found as far back as the late-19th-

century. This was a broken stone, found in a well or cistern in David's City (South

of Temple Mount) with carved decorative elements from a building.

It is translated:

"Theodotus, son of Vettenus, priest and ruler of the synagogue (archisynagogus) son

of a ruler of a synagogue (archisynagogus) and grandson of a ruler of a synagogue

(archisynagogus) built the synagogue for the reading of the Law and the teaching of

the commandments, and also the guest chamber and the upper rooms and the ritual

pools for accommodating those needing them from abroad, which his fathers, the

*elders and Simonides founde*d" (translation in Runesson, Binder and Olsson, The

Ancient Synagogue from its Origins to 200 C.E., A Source Book [2008], 53.)

This

Greek inscription, which was found very close to the Temple, is now a basic item in scholars' consideration of the issue of synagogues. The stone indicates that

Theodotus was the third generation of hereditary leaders of his synagogue. It is also

important to note that Theodotus's father was a priest (of the Temple) while he also

led the synagogue and he obviously brought up his son to carry on the family

tradition.

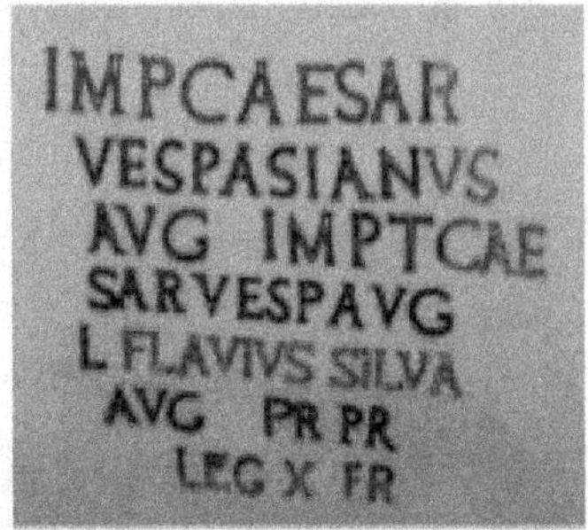

Plate 3.2. The Roman Text.
Photo: Ian Finnin, 2018.

This synagogue was clearly an extensive, multi-storey building but was probably

destroyed by the Romans in 70 C.E. meaning that one or other version of it was standing during 'the Jesus period'. The inscription indicates

that hospitality for travellers and pilgrims, and provisions for ritual purification,

were functions of the Theodotus synagogue but its main purposes were Bible reading

and instruction in Torah observance, which is exactly what Jesus did in synagogues

throughout Galilee.

3) The 10th Legion Inscriptions

Two separate copies of a Latin inscription were set up on columns in Jerusalem by

the 10th Legion Fretensis when it was stationed in the ruined Old City from 70 C.E.

until after Hadrian rebuilt Jerusalem as a Roman city called Colonia Aelia Capitolina

in about 130 C.E.

In 70 C.E. Jerusalem had been unable to withstand the Roman army's onslaught.

With great slaughter the 10th Legion under L. Flavius Silva took Jerusalem, and

established its headquarters near Jaffa Gate for many years. Both inscriptions were

recently discovered near Temple Mount.

The text is translated by Gichon and Isaac, 'A Flavian Inscription', IEJ 24.2

(1974), 117-128:

"Emperor, Caesar Vespasian Augustus, and Emperor Titus Caesar son of Vespasian

Augustus. L. Flavius Silva 10th Legion Fretensis."

The name of L. Flavius Silva, the praetorian prefect of Judea, who had efficiently

led the troops against Jerusalem (and also against Herod's fortress on Massada) was

defaced on both inscriptions. If the local Jews had defaced the inscription they would

have also defaced the reference to the legion, 'LEG X FR', so the damage may have

been official removal of his name when he fell from favour (which was called

damnatio memoriae). In any case these two inscriptions attest to the Roman

destruction of Jerusalem.

Plate 3.3. 'To the Place of Trumpeting' inscription.
Photo: Ian Finnin, 2018.

4) The Two 'Warning to Gentiles' Inscriptions

In the Jewish Temple a one metre high wall of partition, called the Soreg/Shoreg,

delineated the point in the Temple courts past which gentiles could not go. Two

Greek inscriptions, found in 1871 and 1938,

warned gentiles not to trespass in the wrong places. These inscriptions are both

translated:

"No foreigner is to enter within the bulistrade and enclosure around the Temple

area. Whoever is caught will have himself to blame for his death, which will ensue"

(Tim Dowley [ed.], Discovering the Bible [1986], 125.)

5) The 'Place of Trumpeting' Inscription

Another stone artefact that has survived from Herod's Temple is inscribed in Hebrew

and translates as *"to the place of trumpeting"*. This treasure was found among debris

that fell from the South-West corner of Herod's Temple near Robinson's Arch in 70

C. E. It identified the point from which the shofar was sounded in the pre-destruction

Temple at the start and ending of each Sabbath (H. Shanks, Jerusalem's Temple

Mount [2007], 91).

6) Hadrian's Inscription on The Gate of the Pillar

The Arabs call the Damascus Gate "Bab Al-Amud" - Gate of the Pillar - because of

the 2nd century gate beneath it.

This arched, Roman gate does have the visible remains of two pillars (on either side)

but it began life simply as one of the two smaller gates that flanked the, now lost,

larger central gate. The name "Gate of the Pillar" has, however, a more interesting

origin, which becomes clear with a look at the 6th Century Madaba Map (Plate 3.5).

It shows that Emperor Hadrian's grand street-plan had two colonnaded Cardo's sweeping across the city. These both originated at a central plaza just inside

Hadrian's once grand three-arched commemorative gate. Central to this plaza was a

tall column, which supported a statue of Hadrian himself. It can be easily noted on

the Madaba Map, although the statue is not shown.

On the exterior wall of the Gate of the Column an inscription bears the Roman name,

`Colonia Aelia Capitolina'. In 131 AD Emperor Hadrian built this Roman city on the

ruins that Titus had left after destroying Jerusalem in 70 C.E. The city was given that

Roman name to denoted three things:

(1) that Hadrian accorded it the status of a Roman colony, (2) that it was the personal

creation of Hadrian whose family name was Aelius and (3) that the city was

dedicated to the gods of the Capitoline Hill of Rome, whose temple now stood on

Temple Mount. They were Jupiter Capitolina, his wife, Juno, and his daughter

Minerva.

Plate 3.4. Gate of the Pillar. Photo: Justin Campbell, 2019.

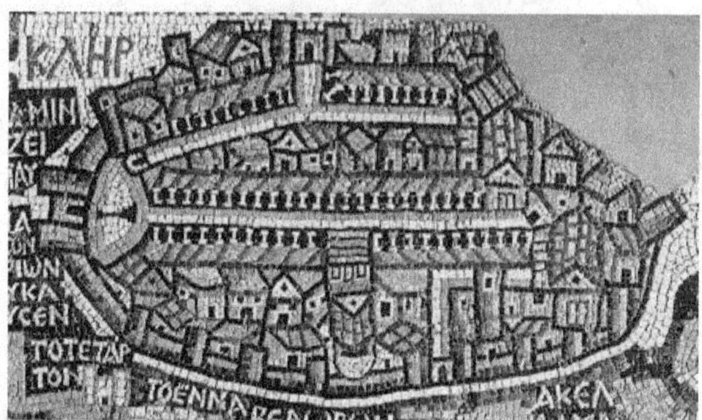

Plate 3.5. Madaba Map, Madaba, Jordan, showing column
and paved plaza to left. Public domain.

and paved plaza to left. Public domain.

In 330 A.D., upon his conversion to Christianity, the
Emperor Constantine restored

the Biblical name `Jerusalem'. Today the gate, the Roman tower and Roman

pavement (now underground) are part of a museum.

7) The Upside Down Inscription at the Double Gates

Plate 3.6. Double Gate (centre in shadow)
Photo: D.Campbell, 1988.

At the southern end of Temple Mount are some interesting stone items.

First the Huldah Steps, restored from 1968 onwards, and secondly the sealed up

Triple Gate and the Double Gate. The latter is partly concealed by a building but

beside the top of the gate that can be seen there is a stone inscribed in Latin. It is

placed upside-down in secondary use.

It names the Emperor Hadrian (117-138 C.E.) and his adopted son Antoninus Pius

(138-161 C.E.) so it must date from the latter's reign and may once have identified

his statue; perhaps even an equestrian statue on Temple Mount. The translation

provided by Hershel Shanks, in Jerusalem's Temple Mount (2007), 48, reads:

TO THE EMPEROR CAESAR
TITUS AELIUS HADRIANUS
ANTONINUS AUGUSTUS PIUS
FATHER OF THE FATHERLAND, PONTIFEX AUGUR
BY THE DECREE OF THE DECURIONS

8) Inscription at the south door of Holy Sepulchre

Plate 3.7. Painting of Holy Sepulchre by David Roberts. Public domain.

Since it was built in c.335 by the Emperor Constantine I the Church of the Holy

Sepulchre has undergone many repairs and revisions because of accidental damage

and deliberate destruction. The South façade and the general layout largely date from

the Crusader period although the square clock tower was originally five storey's high

(in 1248) and both of the graceful main doors facing the courtyard to thhe south

by David Roberts) its large dome over the burial place (the Anastasis or

Resurrection) and the smaller dome, over the Catholicon, are visible.

Above one of the two front doors there is a 12th century Latin inscription translated:

"This place is holy, sanctified by the blood of Christ,
By our consecration we add nothing to its holiness.
But the house built around and above this sacred place
We consecrated on the fifteenth day of July,
With our fathers present, by Fulcher the patriarch,
Who was in the fourth year of his patriarchate,
The fiftieth year since the capture of the City,

Which then shone like pure gold.
From the birth of the Lord there were numbered
Eleven hundred and forty-nine years."

[Martin Biddle, The Tomb of Christ, 1999, 94.]

9) The 6th Century Nea Church Inscription

The Byzantine Christian Emperor Justinian (527-565 CE) was known to have built

a very large and magnificent church overlooking the Temple. It was dedicated to the

Virgin Mary and was called the New Church of the Mother of God (the 'Nea Church'

for short) but it had disappeared without a trace until June 1970. Then evidence of a

very large structure was found. In 1973 and 1983 further evidence was revealed

including its subterranean vaults that served as a cistern.

The climax of the investigation was the discovery, on a barely accessible wall-space

of this dark, watery hiding-place, of a tabula ansata with a Geek inscription. Tsafrir

provided this translation:

"And this is the work which our most pious Emperor Flavius Justinianus carried out

with munificence, under the care and devotion of the most holy Constantius, Priest

and Hegumen, in the thirteenth indiction."

(N. Avigad, 'The Nea', in Tsafrir (ed.), Ancient Churches Revealed (1993), 134.

This inscription confirmed that Justinian's magnificent Nea Church had indeed been found and that it conformed to the description provided in the 6th century by

Justinian's contemporary, Procopius, in his book, Buildings.

Discussion

These important inscribed stones provide important evidence about some of the key

features of Jerusalem's history and its chronology. While both material that can be

Carbon Dated and pottery styles are more indicative of chronology, epigraphers can

also date the writing style and the language used in inscriptions for this purpose, but

a dated inscription (such the one in Holy Sepulchre) is pure gold.

Chapter 4
Walls

The present walls of the Old City of Jerusalem were constructed by the Sultan

Suliman the Magnificent between 1537 and 1542 but some of the foundations, and

the stonework, dates back to the Roman wall built by the Emperor Hadrian in about

130 C.E. Along the western section of the city wall is a piece that is remarkable as

it reveals the various ages and stages of construction.

Starting from the top: the battlements were built in the time of the Turkish Emperor

Suleiman I in the 17th century. The circular decorations of the face of the towers are

Islamic. Although the top is level the various lower strata are not, in fact stones from

various periods are haphazardly used during repairs. Rough bulbous stones are

visible, often with relatively smooth margins all around. There are characteristic of

the Hasmonean period (2nd-1st century B.C.). An occasional Herodian stone can be

found (from the 1st century B.C.). These are very neat stones, precise in shape. The

faces of these stones have a narrow smooth margin on all four sides and a smooth, neat boss.

The Islamic period wall did not exactly follow the Constantinian wall, which was

built in c.324 C.E. Rough elements of an ancient wall can be seen, and even bedrock.

The signage indicates eleven layers, in total.

Plate 4.2. A view from the ramparts. Photo: Justin Campbell, 2019.

There is a spot in the road that winds from the coast inland to Jerusalem where you

experience the thrill of unexpectedly coming upon a brief but breathtaking vista of

beautiful Jerusalem by day, or perhaps of its twinkling night lights which sparkle in

the clear desert air beneath cloudless skies. Never the less it comes as something of

a shock, after driving through modern suburbs, to be confronted suddenly by the

massive austere stones of ancient Jerusalem's towering walls, which are so close to

the road that one momentarily fears a collision. First impressions are not always

lasting impressions and Jerusalem's walls seem less formidable with familiarity.

Their ever-changing colours, moods and character become increasingly intriguing

and their lofty parapets and interesting staircases beg to be explored.

There was a time when climbing on the city walls was a hazardous but inexpensive

pastime. Now it has become commercialised, more organised, but certainly safer. It

remains, however, a pleasure not to be missed. The bird's eye views of the Old City's

various quarters are fascinating, as is the passing parade of people below. But what

is even more fascinating is the experience of standing where history has been written.

History has been made on these very ramparts since the sixteenth century, and on

the site of the city of Jerusalem, for four thousand years, at least.

There is a place where the parapet widens out and a plaque informs the intrepid wall-

explorer that, in 1967, during the Six Day War, Jordanian soldiers fired on New

Jerusalem form this guard post. The tiny people below do seem very vulnerable from

this vantage point.

In the East, the Mount of Olives can be seen in the distance, perhaps catching the

rays of the setting sun; and to the South-East the Y.M.C.A. Tower, Montefiores

Windmill and many modern hotels can easily be seen. Perhaps from odd vantage
points one can view, from above, one of the numerous archaeological ruins which
surround the city walls, both within the city and outside of it.
There are usually some interesting people to encounter during the exploration. The
rarefied atmosphere on the city's ramparts seems to create friends out of total
strangers. People from every corner of the globe can be found here, contemplating,
praying, chatting or quietly looking. Each is making a personal discovery about this
unique and mysteriously attractive city.
The motto used by the Israeli Tourist Bureau to encourage walking on the walls is,
naturally enough, from the Tanach; from one of the Songs of the Sons of Korah,
from the Book of Psalms:
"Walk about Zion, go round her, count her towers, consider well her ramparts, view
her citadels that you may tell of them to the next generation." (Ps. 48:12-13)
These words indicate that the very act of walking around and upon the city walls is
older than these walls themselves and that the spiritual dimension experienced by
the participant has a Divine purpose, it is part of a Divine plan. The entire experience,

its physical and its spiritual aspects, enable the explorer to tell succeeding

generations both the facts, and their significance. This experience is indeed a part of

the mystique that is the essence of Jerusalem.

Jerusalem, the City of Gold, is like no other city on earth. Not the least remarkable

is the effect that it has upon people: both residents and visitors; tourists and pilgrims;

the religious and the secular; the cynical and the sensitive. It seems that no one goes

from this city unchanged.

One other remarkable thing about Jerusalem is its very existence. Not only has it

been systematically destroyed over forty times in its chequered history, but there is

little reason for a city to be there at all. It is neither on a major river, nor a major

trade route. It is not a port, nor is it in a strategic position. It has no natural resources

and is in a remote wilderness locale. Yet God has decreed that it shall remain. The

message contained in Jerusalem's fortifications, and in her continued existence,

despite every imaginable assault, is that God is within those same fortresses and

citadels. They picture His strength and His commitment to this city, His city.

"It is beautiful in its loftiness, the joy of the whole earth. Like the utmost heights of (the North) is Mount Zion the city of the Great King. God is in her citadels; he has

shown himself to be her fortress." (Ps. 48:2-3)

Plate 4.3. Walls, tower and minaret, David's Citadel.
Photo: D. Campbell, 1988.

A post card is sold which pictures an aerial view of the city
- bathed in a golden
     light. The card reads that ancient legend claims that God's
Spirit hovers over the city.

If we turn to the Scriptures we can test this `legend'. Is it historically accurate,

prophetic of the future, or substantiated today? Perhaps it is all three ?

"Since the Lord, the God of Israel has granted rest to his people and (He) has come

to dwell in Jerusalem for ever" (I Chron. 23:25).

Chapter 5

Ancient Gates

When the psalmist speaks of Zion's citadels, which are to be viewed (Ps. 48: 12-13)

the Medieval word 'keep' could be used. The keep or citadel is a more heavily

fortified part of the city previously mentioned, whose defences are independent of

the city's walls and can withstand assault longer than the main city walls.

One such part of Herod's Jerusalem was the Antonia Fortress, built by the puppet

king Herod I beside the Temple. On the other side of the city, to the West the triple

towers of Phasel, Hippicus and Mariamne, built by Herod beside his own palace,

would have been heavily fortified. We know this from the fact that they have

withstood the ravages of the centuries and were incorporated at a later date into the

structure, near the Jaffa Gate, which is known today as David's Citadel. (Its Ottoman-

period minaret can be seen in Plates 4.2. and 6.3.). This fortress was a soldiers'

barracks when Titus billeted the Tenth Legion there. It has housed Moors, Saracens,

Crusaders, Mamelukes and Turks. Today it is a tourist complex and an extensive

museum.

Returning to the Scripture: "Walk about Zion, go round her, count her towers,

consider well her ramparts, view her citadels that you may tell of them to the next

generation." (Ps. 48:12-13). Ancient city gates were usually towers set into the walls,

so "counting the towers" would include counting the gates. In fact some of

Jerusalem's current Old City Gates are also towers: Damascus Gate, Herod's Gate,

Jaffa Gate, Lion's Gate and the Golden Gate. Others, New Gate, Dung Gate and

Tanners Gate, are simply holes in the wall.

Ancient gates were more than entrances to the city, they were places of government,

commerce and the law. In ancient times gates symbolised security, power, and social

concourse. Legal, commercial and administrative decision-making often took place

in the city gates (see Ruth 4:1). Such gates can be seen at Tel Hazor, Meggido and

Gezer.

Ancient gates were elaborate structures, strongly fortified, not mere doors in the

wall. Much thought and expense went into protecting these breaches in the walls, which were by nature the most vital, but vulnerable places in the city. For example,

in Ancient Meggido overlooking the plains of Jezreel, which is one of the most blood

stained battle-fields on earth, the gate was protected by side towers and by a ʻUʼ

shaped apron of wall in front of the main gate, which itself was fortified by towers.

The opening of this apron was in the side, so that chariots and cavalry would find

passage difficult, having to make a 90 degree turn in a confined space. This is a fine

example of attempts to reduce the vulnerability of the city entrance.

City gates that protruded from the wall enabled guards on the ramparts above to see
more clearly in three directions. Flanking towers added strength, with their mass of
masonry, and enabled enclosed stairwells on either sides to provide quick access
above for archers.

In the Middle East preventing mounted troops from entering has been a problem
right into the 20th century. In Jerusalem many buildings and compounds have a
small wicket-gate "the eye of the needle", which enable the larger main gate to
remain shut for added security. Herod's Gate in the Old City illustrates this
precaution.

The entrance to the Church of the Holy Nativity in Bethlehem was partly sealed by
the Crusaders in order to prevent horsemen riding in, so even today adults must still
stoop to enter. Now that gate is called "the Gate of Humility".

Most towered gates had heavy doorways at both front and back openings and in
some cases these openings were not aligned opposite each other. This created an 'L'
shaped passageway, as in the Jaffa Gate (Plate 6.3.), or perhaps a 'Z' shaped
passageway, such as in the Damascus Gate (Plate 6.5.).

In most cases towers are also either a gate or a citadel, but there is an occasional

need for a tower to be built as an observation post or to provide extra strength at a

vulnerable point, such as at the corners of the city. A Corner Gate is mentioned in

Zechariah, where, in Chapter 14, the cities boundaries are defined by listing three

gates: the Corner Gate, First Gate and Benjamin Gate.

Nehemiah Chapter 3 lists some ten of Jerusalem's gates: Dung, Valley, Fountain,

Sheep, Fish, Horse, Old, Water, East and Inspection Gates while Jeremiah mentions

a New Gate. Matthew's Gospel identified two gates but the Gate Beautiful was

within the Temple complex. South of the Temple, the Water Gate overlooked the

Kidron Valley, or Valley of Jehoshaphat (Josaphat) near the Gihon Spring. Of the

many gates which existed long ago at least the Dung Gate (Neh. 2:13), the Hulda

Gates and the Golden Gate have remained in the same position for many centuries:

the Golden Gate because the Eastern Wall of Temple Mount is fixed by the steep

Kidron Valley (Plate), the Huldah Gates because they abut the massive Temple

platform (Plates and) and the Dung Gate because the deep valley to the South was

the best place for landfill.

The key purposes in the designing of walls and gates were protection for citizens

and soldiers, the ability to control entry and exit and increasing defensive

capabilities.

Chapter 6
Gates Today

From the Psalms we know of the Lord's great affection for Jerusalem's gates. "For

the Lord loves the gates of Zion: more than the dwellings of Jacob" (Ps. 87:2). We

are told that Jerusalem's walls, which encompass her, and therefore symbolise the

city in its entirety, are never out of the Lord's mind: "I will not forget you! See, I

have engraved you on the palms of my hands; your walls are ever before me." (Is.

49:6)

Though some of the city's walls and many of her gates are now in different locations

we know that these Scriptures remain true: Jerusalem remains, and will remain in its

place, and Temple Mount stands where it has always stood.

Plate 6.2. Dung Gate, widened for vehicles. Public domain.

To `count

her towers' and to 'consider her ramparts' mean to pay attention to her

defences, or, as the Authorised Version puts it, to 'mark well her bulwarks'. Before

considering any spiritual interpretation of the admonition from Psalm 48:12 to

consider her ramparts, citadels and towers it is appropriate to survey the present city

gates and to commence with a gate whose stones have changed but whose name and

function has remained with us since Biblical times.

1) DUNG GATE

The Dung Gate, south of the city, was so named because refuse was taken through

it to be thrown into the deep ravine of the Valley of Hinnom, or Gehenna. Continual

fires burnt in this valley of garbage, which gave rise to the association of Hades with

Gehenna and with fire. This valley, now much filled in, runs to the East and the

South of the city from the Jaffa Gate to the Pool of Siloam where it joins the Kidron

Valley in a 'Y' shaped junction just near the Dung Gate. Today the Dung Gate, once

just a hole in the wall, is a security check point and bustling major entrance to the

area around the Western Wall and the entrance to Temple Mount for non-Muslims.

Plate 6.2. Zion Gate. Public domain.

2) TANNERS GATE

Moving in a clockwise direction, the next gate is Tanners Gate. This is both an

ancient and a new gate: ancient because it was built by the Crusaders in the 12th

century and new because it was blocked up for hundreds of years and only reopened

recently. It is a narrow hole in the wall and is strictly for pedestrians as the approach

is via a narrow walkway, elevated above ruined cisterns, mikvahot (ritual baths), a

Crusader tower and eight Byzantine Era paving stones.

3) ZION GATE

The next gate, Zion Gate, was built in 1540 to provides access to the hill presently

called Mount Zion, with its important Christian buildings. The Arabs call it "Prophet

David's Gate", because David is traditionally associated with Mt Zion and because

his tomb is nearby. David's city, Orphel, is however closer to the Dung Gate, and is

outside the mid-16th century walls of Suleiman the Magnificent.

Unfortunately Suleiman's walls exclude modern Mount Zion and David's city,

whereas in previous times both Orphel and Mt Zion were encircled within the city

walls. The Old City's boundaries have changed a number of times, although Temple

Mount has always been the dominant feature.

Plate 6.3. Jaffa Gate (centre) is dwarfed by the towers and minaret of David's Citadel (to the rear). Photo: Justin Campbell, 2019.

Zion Gate is a projecting tower with an internal stone stairwell leading to guard

rooms and an observation roof. It has inner and outer recessed arched portals,

battlements and Ottoman decorations on the exterior wall. Other interesting

'ornamentations' are the many bullet holes made in 1948 during the unsuccessful

defence of the Jewish Quarter whose 1300 residents fled to the New City through

this gate. Many small boys ran through it, clutching precious Torah scrolls rescued

from the Quarter's fifty-eight synagogues, which were soon to be deliberately

desecrated or destroyed by the Jordanian invaders.

4) JAFFA GATE

As seen in Plate 6.3., Jaffa Gate projects out from the line of the city wall and is very

close to David's Citadel. Jaffa Gate has embrasures and stone turrets and an `L'

shaped passageway. This prevented vehicle entry so in 1898 a large hole was cut

into the wall nearby to permit the entry of the royal carriage of Kaiser Wilhelm of

Prussia (although he rode in on a white horse).

The Arabs call Jaffa Gate "Bab El Khatil" - Gate of the Friend, perhaps because

Abraham, the friend of God, with his son (Isaac or Ishmael, depending upon whether one is Jewish or Muslim), would have approached Mount Moriah (Temple Mount),

from this point on his way to the fateful sacrifice. Some Arabs, however, believe that

the name is connected with Hebron, where Abraham is buried.

Plate 6.4. New Gate. Public domain.

As noted in the previous entry, David's Tomb is not included within the city walls.

It is said that Suleiman executed his two architects for this oversight and that the two

Islamic-style graves inside Jaffa Gate are theirs.

5) NEW GATE

This simple gate in the Jewish Quarter is merely a door in the wall, built in 1889, at

a time when strong fortifications were becoming unnecessary. New Gate is also

called "Gate of the Sultan" because it was built by the Ottoman Sultan Abdul Hamid

II (1876-1908) to provide access to the new areas being built outside the city

enclosure.

6) DAMASCUS GATE

The Damascus Gate is Suleiman the Magnificent's masterpiece as it is both the

largest and the most ornate. Its walls are sixteen metres high and for extra security

it has two side towers and battlements that protected soldiers above. The Ottoman-

style pinnacled battlements add an air of grace to the outer facade. Its vaulted internal

chamber is quite dark because of the staggered passageway, and there is the

traditional provision for market stalls within and around the its opening

Plate 6.5. Damascus Gate. Photo: Justin Campbell, 2019.

It is sometimes called the Gate of Shechem" because the road to Shechem (Nablus)

begins here.

7) HERODS GATE

This gate set into a projecting tower is in the North wall of the old city and it gives

access to the city's Moslem Quarter. It has had many names, including "Flowers

Gate", which may have resulted from an error in pronunciation.

Its projecting tower has plain battlements and minimal decoration and the opening

above the doorway was created to permit hot tar or oil to be

poured down upon attackers at the doorway although originally the opening was in

a side wall. As in the Jaffa Gate, this created an `L' shaped passage-way which did

not allow for the easy passage of hortses, carts and small vehicles. The present

opening is in the front of this austere tower, which has a small wicket-gate set into

its timber doorway.

8) LIONS GATE

The two pairs of sculpted lions (panthers) on the exterior facade give Lions Gate its

most memorable name but, since the time of the Crusades, Christians have also

called this gate "St Stephen's Gate" and prior to that it was called "St Mary's Gate" because her tomb site is nearby. The Crusaders associated this area with the death of

Stephen, the first Christian martyr, who was dragged outside a city gate and stoned

to death (see Acts 7:58) but the original memorial church, built by Empress Eudocia

Plate 6.6. Herods Gate or Flowers Gate. Public domain.

in the 5th century was outside Damascus Gate. One column from it stands on the

site, now in the grounds of L'Ecolé Biblique.

Lions Gate is to the East of the city, facing the Mount of Olives, at the end of the

Via Doloroso, the traditional Way of the Cross. It has an arched portal and an inner

gate and battlements above. The lions began life as emblems of the Mamluke Sultan

Baibars and were reused by Suleiman when he renovated the gate.

In 1967 Israeli soldiers entered through it to liberate the Old City, and the Western

Wall, from Jordanian control.

Plate 6.7. Lions or St Stephen's Gate, c.1867. Public domain.

9) GOLDEN GATE

By far the most fascinating gate is the sealed Golden Gate whose destiny was

foretold by scriptures long ago.

"..the outer gate of the sanctuary, the one facing east, and it was shut. The lord said

to me, `This gate is remain shut. It must not be opened ; no-one may enter through

it.'" (Ez. 44:2)

The Golden Gate faces the Mount of Olives as though silently but expectantly

awaiting the return of the one of whom it was said: "On that day his feet will stand

on the Mount of Olives, east of Jerusalem, and the Mount of Olives will be split in

two." (Zech.13:4)

For many reasons this gate is unique: for the legend and mystery which surrounds

it: because of the mysterious and inaccessible arched gate which lies buried

immediately below it surrounded by a mass of human skeletons; because of its

proximity to the site of the Temple; because of its intimate association with Jesus

and with the Garden of Gethsemane nearby; because it faces the place of Jesus'

ascension; and because of the prophetic scriptures which reveal its sublime future.

This gate, with its

beautiful twin arches of Repentance and Mercy, will once again be opened, and it

will have a beautiful future role.

Plate 6.8. The Golden Gate in 1900. Pulic domain.

Plate 6.9. Rear view of the Golden Gate. Photo: D. Campbell, 1994.

"I saw the glory of the God of Israel coming from the east
..... The glory of the Lord

entered the temple through the gate facing east." (Ez. 43:1&4)

Plate 6.10. Sealed Golden Gate facing East. Photo: Ian Finnin, 2018.

The Golden Gate faces the Mount of Olives as though silently but expectantly

awaiting the return of the one of whom it was said: "On that day his feet will stand

on the Mount of Olives, east of Jerusalem, and the Mount of Olives will be split in

two." (Zech.13:4)

For many reasons this gate is unique: for the legend and mystery which surrounds

it: because of the mysterious and inaccessible arched gate which lies buried

immediately below it surrounded by a mass of human skeletons; because of its

proximity to the site of the Temple; because of its intimate association with Jesus

and with the Garden of Gethsemane nearby; because it faces the place of Jesus' ascension; and because of the prophetic scriptures which reveal its sublime future.

This gate, with its beautiful twin arches of Repentance and Mercy, will once again

be opened, and it will have a beautiful future role.

"I saw the glory of the God of Israel coming from the east ..... The glory of the Lord

entered the temple through the gate facing east." (Ez. 43:1&4)

10) THE SHUT GATES

**Plate 6.11. Part of the double gate, in the corner.
Photo: Ian Finnin, 2018.**

Thus far the principal gates have been numbered: eight in all. There remain the

sealed gates, all of which are in the Temple Mount area (and which include the

Golden Gate). Four of them, in the western face of Temple Mount, are named after

modern explorers who discovered them: Robinson, Warren, Wilson and Barclay.

The most important are the Huldah Gates in the South, which may have been named

after the revered prophetess Huldah. The Huldah Gates include the double portal

(Plate 6.11.) and the tipple-arched portal (Plate 6.12.). They are connected by the

Huldah Steps, an external staircase dating from Herod's Temple. These stairs were excavated in the late 20th century and have been restored more recently, as Plate

6.12. shows. They were the usual public exit and entryway for Temple Mount before

the destruction of 70 C.E. and would have been well known to Jesus and his

followers. The triple gates are Islamic but based on Herodion precursors, although

only one stone of Plate 6.12., a part of the western doorjamb, is Herodion [Bahat, in

Charlesworth, 43].

Plate 6.12. Triple Arches and restored Huldah Steps.
Photo: D. Campbell, 2013.

Plate 6.13. South wall of the Temple Platform. Photo: Ian Finnin, 2018.

The Huldah Gates lead into chambers within the Temple Mount platform, where
internal steps go up onto the platform. The Crusader Knights Templar used a very

large underground chamber as a horse stable. Its roof is (or was) supported by eighty-

eight huge pillars and it was known as Solomon's Stables because it was thought to

date back to Solomon's Temple (the First Temple). In fact it dates from the period

of Herod's Temple. Recently it has been reconfigured as an underground mosque.

The repaired pale patch of wall (top right of Plate 6.13) is evidence of damage caused

during the building of the mosque when the wall bulged out dangerously, until

engineers were sent from Jordan to successfully repair it.

Chapter 7
Spiritual Defences

Spiritually speaking each person, no matter what his occupation or status must

contribute to Jerusalem's defences. Each must be a watchman, part of her guard

network, though some, like the nobles of Tekoa, in Nehemiah's day refuse to help.

Nehemiah Chapter Two tells us that families and neighbours worked together

repairing the walls of Jerusalem. Shallum, who was a regional ruler in the city, was

assisted in his repair task by his daughters. the Levites who served in the Lord's

Temple worked together. Co-operative work was carried out by men of cities, such

as Mizpah and Gibeon, while some workers repaired near their homes and others

went where the need was greatest. Each assisted until, despite the opposition from

their enemies, the task, which took just fifty-two days, was completed. What each

could not achieve alone, the group could achieve by working together. The lesson

for us today in this is obvious: there are many advantages, in spiritual matters, as in

the purely physical, in joint effort and mutual support.

Nehemiah recorded that there came a day when the gates and the walls were

completed, secure and ready to be dedicated. For this celebration the people were

recalled from their home-towns. Those who played the lyre, harp, cymbals and

trumpet gathered, along with hundreds of singers. On that joyful day, when the city

was rededicated to the Lord, two great choirs, each followed by half of the people,

encircled the city upon the ramparts, in opposite directions. They all met in the

Temple, to bring their sacrifices, and to praise the Holy One of Israel.

"On that day they offered great sacrifices because God had given them great joy.

The women and children also rejoiced. The sound of rejoicing in Jerusalem could be

heard far away." (Neh.12:43)

This was a day for a new beginning, marked by purity and its companion, joy. "When

the priests and Levites had purified themselves ceremonially, they purified the

people, the gates and the wall." (Neh. 12:30)

There is, therefore, a wonderful scriptural precedent for singing upon Jerusalem's

walls and encircling the city with the Lord's praises. Unfortunately this cannot be

wholly done to-day because the ramparts are broken, in part. The major breach in the wall near the Jaffa Gate was made for Kaiser Wilhelm II, in 1898, and never

repaired. It makes it impossible to encircle the Old City, or, for that matter, to close

and secure it. Now "walking all around her" can

only be done at ground level, and that with some difficulty.

reach in Jerusalem's walls is a continual reminder to us of Nehemiah's lament:

" You see the trouble we are in: Jerusalem lies in ruins, and its gates have been

burned with fire. Come, let us rebuild the wall of Jerusalem, and we will no longer

be in disgrace". (Neh.3:17)

In Ancient Times Jerusalem's broken walls were a reproach to the Lord's people. In

our day her protection can only be found in the Holy One, in His might and His will.

Israel cannot trust in horses or chariots, nor even in tanks and aircraft, nor, for that

matter, in American dollars. Today her walls are built, not with stones and mortar

but with prayer and faith: prayer with faith and faith with prayer. Today, any

permanent breach in her walls made of stones is not significant, except to serve as a

reminder, but weaknesses in spiritual defences are critical.

Nehemiah's response to the broken defences of his beloved Jerusalem was to issue

an urgent appeal for help to repair them. Men and women; governor and goldsmith;

perfumer and priest: each responded and zealously worked to repair a small section.

Today there is an urgent call going out from those who especially love this city, and

the land of which it is the heart and symbol, for help in the restoration of its defences,

even small parts of its walls of faith and prayer. A response of willingness and zeal, like that which Nehemiah knew is urgently needed.

While Jerusalem's enemies now have different names they are very similar, in many

ways, to the adversaries who opposed Nehemiah's work. Their aims, to see Israel

physically defenceless, economically crippled, and with her religious life in tatters,

are the same. They still try to deceive and to trap, to harass and to hamper, and, when

these fail, to give an evil report to powerful rulers on the international scene, tactics

which have an all too familiar ring.

In Nehemiah's era, the workers contributed their labour by day, and served as

watchmen by night. So alert for danger did they remain, that guards and watchmen

alike slept in their clothing, with their weapons continually with them. This

illustrates a degree of vigilance that is still required in Israel, as the recent axe murder

of three Israeli soldiers, while sleeping in their tent, shows. Sleeping while on guard

duty remains the most serious of offences known to the I.D.F. and illustrates to us

the need for constant vigilance in the Spirit and an awareness of the needs, the

dangers and the issues. Naivety and ignorance are not signs of spirituality!!

Chapter 8

Weapons of Our Warfare

The offensive and defensive weapons for spiritual warfare are virtually the same.

They are:

(1) The Word of God

(2) The Blood of Jesus

(3) Words of positive confession and testimony

(4) The Name of Jesus

(5) Praise and worship and

(6) in the case of defence, resisting of evil.

There are many Scriptures which both teach and illustrate the use of these weapons.

(1) The Word of God

There is no more fitting example of the use of the Word of God, called `the Sword

of the Spirit', than Jesus' own use of the Hebrew Scriptures (the Tanach) when

tempted by satan.

"Jesus answered, `It is written: Worship the Lord your God and serve him only.'"

(Luk.4:8)

(2&3) The Blood of the Lamb and the Word of their Testimony

The importance of the Blood of Jesus and words of positive testimony are summed up together in words spoken by a voice from heaven, on the island of Patmos, to

John, during his vision :

"For the accuser of our brothers, who accuses them before our God day and night,

has been hurled down. They overcame him by the blood of the Lamb and by the

word of their testimony.." (Rev. 12:11)

St Paul, quoting from Psalm 116, wrote of positive confessions of faith:

"It is written: 'I believe; therefore I have spoken'. With that same spirit of faith we

also believer and therefore speak, because we know that the one who raised the Lord

Jesus from the dead will also raise us with Jesus and bring us with you in his

presence. All this is for your benefit." (II Cor. 4:13-15a)

(4) The Name of Jesus

The Apostles used the Name of Jesus many times in their years of ministry. We have

examples from their healing and deliverance ministries, for example Peter said to a

crippled beggar, at the Gate Beautiful:

"Silver and gold I do not have, but what I have I give you. In the name of Jesus

Christ of Nazareth, walk." (Acts.3:6)

Paul delivered a slave girl from a spirit of divination. Using the power of the Name

of Jesus he addressed the evil spirit:

"In the name of Jesus Christ I command you to come out of her". (Act.16:18)

(5) Praise and Worship

It is from the Tanach, the Old Testament, that we find many examples of praise and

worship being blessed in a mighty way in physical defence. Examples come from

the assault of Jericho by Joshua's men and from the Jehoshaphat's war with Edom,

Moab and Amon (see Jos. 6:12-20 & II Chron. 20:21). In the days of the early

Church miracles attended the prayers and praises of the believers. Many gathered in

Mary and John-Mark's house for prayer after Peter's imprisonment and his

consequent miraculous escape was with angelic assistance (see Acts 12:12). The

example of Paul and Silas is outstanding, as they praised God despite having recently been severely but illegally flogged. Yet again praise was miraculously effective and

this time it led to the conversion of their jailer and his whole household, who had,

presumably, been listening.

"About midnight Paul and Silas were praying and singing hymns to God, and the

other prisoners were listening to them. Suddenly there was such a violent earthquake

that the foundations of the prison were shaken. At once all the prison doors flew

open, and everybody's chains came loose." (Acts 16:26)

Praise is fruitful in three ways:

1) Praise is effective in the affairs of people in the heavenlies because God

dwells in that praise and responds to it

2) Praise effects radical change in those who praise

3) Praise makes satan flee.

(6) The Priestly Anointing

The oil, incense and spices to be used in the Temple were so important that specially

selected Levites were appointed as gatekeepers and given charge of them. These

items had great spiritual significance (I Chron. 10:28-30). Oil was used to light the seven branched oil lamp, the great gold menorah, in the Holy Place (see Ex. 37:17-

23). Oil was also used to anoint kings and priests, setting them aside for holy

purposes, as God commanded:

"Anoint Aaron and his sons and consecrate them so they may serve me as priests.

Say to the Israelites, 'This is to be my sacred anointing oil for the generations to

come.'" (Ex. 30:30-31)

(7) Resist Evil

In defence against the onslaughts of temptation and satanic attack we are

commanded to resist satan, but not in our own strength and willpower. First to submit

the problematic matter and ourselves to the Lord's power and mercy.

"Submit yourselves, then, to God. Resist the devil, and he will flee from you." (Jas.

4:7)

It is most important to turn our attention away from both the tempter and the

temptation, and onto our Sovereign and Redeemer.

It is with these weapons, which we have been given, that the battle is fought and

won.

Chapter 9

Spiritual Significance of the Gates

It is obvious when considering a closed environment like a walled city that almost

everything, good or evil used by and consumed by its citizens must come in from

outside, through the gates. Weapons enter secretly while wheat for the daily bread

enters openly through the gates. Things which are not of themselves bad, but which

can have a detrimental effect on the inhabitants, enter through these entrances, so

gates must be used as a means of restricting, controlling or preventing entry. This is

the task of the gatekeeper.

City gates today are hard to define - air waves and telephone lines are as much a part

of our gates as airports and central rail stations. By these means evil secretly sneaks

into, or floods into, our modern cities without hindrance, and our family and

community walls are mostly undefended.

When Nehemiah was able to shut the gates and secure the city by night he was able

to strengthen the spiritual life of the nation by insisting that Gentile merchants and traders refrained from selling their wares on the Sabbath. It was only having to spend

entire nights at the locked gates that convinced these Gentiles that it was useless to

come on the Sabbath in the future. Indecisiveness on Nehemiah's part would have

lost the day as these merchants were as strongly motivated by the prospects of profit

as, for example, the tobacco lobby in our society is today.

Nehemiah was able to stand his ground because he knew that, as a ruler, he was

responsible for the moral and spiritual character of the people and that observance

of Shabbat (the Sabbath) was enshrined in God's Law and was His will for the whole

city corporately and each person individually.

"Once or twice the merchants and sellers of all kinds of goods spent the night outside

Jerusalem. But I warned them and said, 'Why do you spend the night by the wall? If

you do this again I will lay hands on you.'" (Neh.13:2-21)

By comparison with Nehemiah, our community leaders often make a very half-

hearted attempt to control corporate or individual moral virtue. They permit

damaging material and dangerous substances through the gates of our nations

seemingly unhindered. Similarly the spiritual life and purity of the nation is ravaged if the watchmen and gate-keepers are not vigilant, or are ignorant of their role.

Chapter 10

Gatekeepers

The roles of gatekeeper and watchman are different, although their tasks may

overlap. These two offices were generally performed by different people, one on the

walls and the other below, as in Nehemiah's day. Thus the spiritual duties performed

today by watchmen and gatekeepers may differ, and yet be complimentary and

similar.

Gate-keeping was often a humble task. Even sheepfolds had a gatekeeper: not a very

grand occupation, but an important one for the sheep-owner and the shepherd. The

security of the animal enlosure was in the gatekeeper's hands and he knew the

identity of those who were permitted entry.

"He who enters by the door (into the sheep-fold) is the shepherd of the sheep. To

him the gatekeeper opens..." (Jn. 10: 2-3a)

To be a gatekeeper in the Lord's Temple was a very worthy task, but a still relatively

humble role.

"I would rather be a doorkeeper in the house of the Lord than dwell in the tents of

the wicked." (Ps. 84:10b)

Gatekeepers at the Temple had to sleep in the precincts because the gates had to be

opened at first light to permit entry to those who wished to worship early. They and

the singers who praised the Lord within the Temple received their livelihood from

gifts brought to the Temple treasuries. It was a great privilege to open up the House

of the Lord, to facilitate worship, to greet the devout waiting at the gate and those

who came to offer sacrifices and to greet a new day in the Lord's House and to hear

the first chords of praise by the musicians and singers.

Even today there are gatekeepers who sleep within the towers at various gates: at

schools, churches and institutions around the city, for the security of the people

within, and so that the gate can be readily opened when needed.

Before his death, King David appointed four thousand gatekeepers and four

thousand musicians, all from among the tribe of Levi (I Chron. 23:5). These roles

were regarded as sacred offices, which required personal purity according to the

customs laid down by David and Solomon (see Neh. 12:44-47).

In Scripture, one of the most beautiful and sacred tasks of the gatekeeper was that allotted to four heads of Levitical families when Solomon's magnificent Temple was finally completed. They were appointed to guard and care for the Temple

treasures, carefully accounting for them each day.

"The four principal gatekeepers; who were Levites, were entrusted with the

responsibilities for the rooms and treasures in the House of God... Some of them

were in charge of the articles used in the Temple service; they counted them when

they were brought in and when they were taken out." (I Chron. 9:26 & 28)

The custodians of the Temple's treasures were given a great weight of

responsibility as the treasures were of priceless monetary value and great

significance. There is a preserved record of how many of them were taken away to

Babylon when Solomon's Temple was looted and destroyed: 30 gold dishes, 1,000

silver dishes, 29 silver pans, 30 gold bowls, 410 matching silver bowls and 1,000

other articles. King Cyrus returned a total of 5,400 vessels of gold and silver to the

Jews when he permitted them to return to Jerusalem after their seventy years of

captivity (Ezra 1:7-9).

As long ago as 1925 the cost of the First Temple was estimated at $US 87 billion.

Today its furnishings and fittings would be priceless. For example, a tiny ivory vessel from that Temple, recently purchased for the Israel Museum, cost half a

million US dollars, while the solid gold menorah which the Temple Institute has

prepared in readiness for the rebuilding of the Temple cost $US10,000,000. This

indicates that the custodians of the treasures bore a great weight of responsibility.

The treasures were also of great cultural and religious significance, not just of

priceless monetary value.

At the city walls the gatekeeper and watchman worked co-operatively. In many

cases the gatekeeper had to trust the judgement of the watchman who was on a

lookout tower or on the ramparts. For the safety of the city the gatekeeper had to

quickly obey the instructions that the watchman called down to him. At other times

the watchman would discern friend or foe at close quarters, so that, on his own

initiative he would open or shut the main gate, or the wicket gate. If he made an

error of judgement the city would be defenceless.

The intercessor is a gate-keeper, by keeping in place a protective wall of prayer.

By withstanding enemy entry he protects the city, or nation, from infiltration.

Perhaps he will need to support wounded or weary warriors returning from the battlefield, as this is a caring, supportive and compassionate role.

Spiritual discernment is essential, because another task of the gatekeeper is to

admit friends and spiritual reinforcements. Most significantly, the gatekeeper must

recognise and give a ready welcome to the King.

To summarise: the role of gatekeeper is a vital but humble task requiring co-

operation, vigilance, obedience, responsibility and holiness.

"Then I commanded the Levites to purify themselves and go and guard the gates in

order to keep the Sabbath day holy." (Neh. 13:22)

Thus the keeping of Jerusalem's gates is a holy duty, a pure duty and a priestly

ministry. Godly and cleansed gatekeepers are required today, to protect the

spiritual purity both of Israel and our nations.

"I rejoiced with those who said to me,

'Let us go up to the house of the Lord,'

Our feet are standing in your gates , O Jerusalem.

Jerusalem is built like a city that is deeply compacted together:

That is where the tribes go up, the tribes of the Lord,

to praise the name of the Lord according to the Statute given to Israel.

There the thrones for judgement stand, the thrones of the house of David."

"Pray for the peace of Jerusalem,

'May those who love you be secure, May there be peace within your walls and

security within your citadels'

For the sake of my brothers and friends, I will say, 'Peace be within you', For the

sake of the house of the Lord our God, I will seek your prosperity." (Ps. 122:1-9,

NIV).

Chapter 11

The Role of the Watchman

First and foremost is the fact that every person, to some degree, has a watchman's

role and responsibility towards Israel, and towards Jerusalem in particular. It is not

the task of a handful, the capable few, a dedicated elite, but of all who "call upon

the Lord".

"You who call upon the Lord, give yourselves no rest, and give him no rest till he

establishes Jerusalem and makes her the praise of the earth," (Is. 62:6b-7)

Couple this with the knowledge that all are called to be watchmen for the Jewish

people both in the land and in the Dispersion – the WHOLE House of Israel, as

well as for themselves, their own families, their church and their nation.

"Son of man, I have made you a watchman for the House of Israel." (Ez. 33:7)

The role of watchman is of great importance, and a heavy responsibility.

"If the watchman sees the sword coming and does not blow the trumpet to warn the

people and the sword comes and takes the life of one of them, that man will be

taken away because of his sin, but I will hold the watchman accountable for his

blood." (Ez. 33:6)

The watchman's role differs from that of the gatekeeper in that the former was

generally more conspicuous to those both inside and outside the city. The

watchman's role was also more prominent and more vocal, involving calling,

shouting, declaring and blowing the ram's horn trumpet, or shofar. It required far

sightedness, and always had a military ingredient, a warrior element, which was

not always required of gatekeepers.

A closer look at the role that the watchman in the walled cities of ancient Israel

performed will indicate aspects of our responsibility as watchmen for Israel, and

for our nations today.

1) The watchman was stationed upon the gate towers and ramparts of the city wall.

"I will stand at my watch and station myself on the ramparts". (Hab. 2:1)

This speaks of being ready, in a high place, the right place, a place of strength and

vision.

2) The watchman was assigned a 'watch' of three or four hours duration and he

had to remain awake and alert.

"Go, post a lookout and have him report what he sees ... let him be alert, fully

alert." (Is. 21:6b-7b

This teaches the need to have a listening ear, to be vigilant and to endure, bearing

inconvenience in order to finish the task.

3) The watchman was to walk on the ramparts, calling out to the other watchmen –

checking that all was well, and reassuring them of his own safety.

"I have posted watchmen on your walls, O Jerusalem; they will never be silent day

or night." (Is. 62:6a)

This speaks of the need for continuous prayer, and for unity, a cooperative

watching, concern for others' welfare and obedience to instructions. Watchmen are

posted on the walls: they are not there by accident. These qualities are especially

important when praying for Israel because of the great intensity of the spiritual battles for Israel, which will be fought, and are being fought, at this crucial period

of cosmic history.

4) The watchman was to keep watch for a messenger from the enemy, or for an

advancing army.

"Son of man speak to your countrymen and say to them 'When I bring the swords

against a land and the people of the land choose one of their men and make him

their watchman, ... he sees the sword coming against the land and blows the

trumpet to warn the people..." (Ez. 33:1-3)

The watchman must know who the enemy is. This Scripture also reinforces the

need for vigilance and for warning others of impending danger – the public and

conspicuous aspects of the watchman's role. Prophetic insight results in prophetic

declaration.

5) The watchman was to order the gate to be opened, to admit citizens, friends and

allies; or to shut it, to exclude intruders, spies or enemies.

"While the gatekeepers are still on duty, make them shut the doors and bar them."

(Neh. 7:3)

This emphasises the watchman's power to protect the people at the point of entry,

the weakest point in the wall; plus the most important task of spiritual discernment, of detecting friend and fore in the spiritual realm. It also emphasises the co-

operative role played by both watchman and gatekeeper.

6) The watchman was to sound the alarm to the citizens, by blowing the horn, or

shofar.

"Blow the trumpet in Zion; sound the alarm on my holy hill. Let all who live in the

land tremble..." (Joel 2:1)

This means that the watchman must loudly publicise the state of danger, the truth

about a threat. Awareness must be raised, an alarm must be urgently, clearly and

unmistakably sounded, so that it will not be ignored.

7) The watchman was to report the arrival of a messenger, with news of victories.

"And the lookout shouted 'Day after day, my lord, I stand on the watchtower;

every night I stay at my post. Look, here comes a man in a has fallen, has fallen!'" (Is. 21: 8-9)

We are to emphasise the Lord's victory, rather than concentrating our attention on

enemy manoeuvres.

8) The watchman was to welcome the king as he returned from battle.

"Listen, your watchmen lift up their voices; together they shout for joy. When the

Lord returns to Zion, they will see it with their own eyes," (Is. 52.8)

Thus the watchman has far sighted vision. He is the first to announce the good

news. His is one of the most exciting and significant roles at this time in history –

watching for and proclaiming the soon return of the King of all the Earth, seeing

the signs of his coming and recognising Him when he comes!

9) The watchman was also a warrior. If the enemy attacked he would remain at his

post and fight. If enemies assaulted the walls he was the first line of defence. If the

wall was breached his body stood in the gap and held off the enemy. Rescue and

deliverance are the tasks of the warrior-watchman.

"They all plotted together to come and fight against Jerusalem and stir up trouble

against it. But we prayed to our God and posted a guard day and night to meet this

threat." (Neh. 4: 8,9)

This affirms the need for endurance, vigilance and steadfastness in the face of

opposition, and, above all, the need to bring our needs to the Lord in prayer, to plead for His Hand of Protection to be over our people, and over Zion.

"Unless the Lord watches over the city, the watchmen stand guard in vain." (Ps. 127:1b)

Chapter 12
Watchman, What of the Night?

If the spiritual watchmen fail to be alert on the walls and at the gates of our

communities the enemy marches in to plunder them spiritually, to take their most

vulnerable and spiritually defenceless citizens captive. The war and the victory, or

defeat, are spiritual.

"For our struggle is not against flesh and blood, but against rulers, against the

authorities, against the powers of this dark world and against the spiritual forces of

evil in the heavenly realms." (Eph. 6:12)

It is plain from Paul's words in this verse that the battle is on an unseen and spiritual

battle-front. All around us today the nations continue to be blinded by evil forces.

Being without a vision, and without a rescuer, they are led into captivity. They are

like Judah's King Hezekiah, whom the Babylonians first blinded and then led away

captive, as the history of the kings of Israel so poignantly describes.

"They killed the sons of Zedekiah before his eyes. The they put out his eyes, bound

him with bronze shackles and took him to Babylon ... (they) carried into exile the

people who remained in the city, along with the rest of the populace and those who

had gone over to the King of Babylon." (II Kng. 25:7,11)

The story of the Babylonian Captivity and the fate of King Zedekiah, whose last

visual memory was the murder of the sons whom he believed would some day reign

in Jerusalem, is very tragic. So also is the fact that great spiritual blindness about the times in which we are living has descended upon much of the Church. Large

numbers are also spiritually blind when it comes to seeing the truths about God's

purposes for Israel: "having eyes

they see not": but the Scriptures urge believers not to be blind, but to seek the miracle

of 'sight', which we may call 'insight'.

"You do not realise that you are wretched, pitiful, poor, blind and naked. I counsel

you to buy from me ... salve to put on your eyes, so that you can see." (Rev. 3:17b,

18b)

There is to be the closest possible communication between the many watchmen upon

the walls of prayer and faith, and between them and the gatekeepers of the gates.

The holy things of the Lord, the precious treasures and truths are to be entrusted to

faithful people who will care for them and pass them on to others. In ancient times

the governor of Jerusalem, Nehemiah, gave his brother Hanani (with Hananiah the

commander of the citadel) charge of the city because Hanani was a man of

integrity who feared God. Similarly, the Apostle Paul advised Timothy: "the things

you have heard me say in the presence of many witnesses entrust to reliable men who will also be qualified to teach others." (II Tim. 2:2). The faithful and mature

saints are to be guardians of the Lord's treasures.

The watchmen are to be on guard to sound warnings both to the nations and to

Israel. "I appointed watchmen over you and said, 'Listen to the sound of the

trumpet!" (Jer. 6:17). The trumpet sounds to warn Israel about enemy activities in

matters of internal and external security, and economic affairs, as well as prophet

warnings from the Lord.

"Son of man I have made you a watchman for the house of Israel; so hear the word

I speak and give them warning from me." (Ez. 33.7)

The watchmen are to warn the nations concerning God's jealous concern for the

Land and her people: "For this is what the Lord Almighty says... 'Whoever

touches you touches the apple of his eye.'" (Zec. 2:8b)

"This is what the Lord Almighty says, 'I am very jealous for Zion; I am burning

with jealousy for her.'" (Zec. 8:1)

Watchmen will declare the Lord's good plans for Israel's future:

"I will remove the sin of this land in a single day". "The Lord will again comfort

Zion and choose Jerusalem." (Zec. 3:9b; 1:17b)

The shofar, or horn of a kosher animal, was the instrument used to sound the alarm, and is a symbol of the voice of the Almighty. The shofar makes a particular sounding called the 'teruah'. It's message is a warning. It struck fear into the hearts

of both citizens, who knew its meaning, and the foe, to whom it was a frightening

portent. The shofar quickly spurred the people into defensive action. "When the

shofar sounds in the city do not the people tremble?" (Amos 3:6a. alt. trans.)

The shofar is also intended to announce to the nations a warning that Israel is not

to be harmed because it is the apple of God's eye. His attitude

to Israel is one of protection and jealousy, and his anger is quickly kindled (Ps.

2:12). Those who harm Israel will not go unpunished in the end.

Proclaim this word: "This is what the Lord Almighty says. 'I am very jealous for

Jerusalem and for Zion, but I am very angry with the nations that feel secure.'"

(Zec. 1:14-15b)

The shofar was also sounded to call the people together for a holy convocation, or

assembly, to gather them unto the Lord God, especially for the Feasts of Trumpets.

This is a sacred day specifically set aside for Sabbath rest and the hearing and

blowing of the shofar, or many of them.

"On the first day of the seventh month you are to have a day of rest, a sacred assembly, commemorated with trumpet blasts." (Lev, 23:24) This is now

celebrated as Jewish New Year (Rosh Hashannah).

Plate 12.2. Shofarot and trumpets on Rosh Hashannah. Photo: D. Campbell.

The shofar is sounded to declare and proclaim the Lord's Sovereignty. In fact one

of the three distinctive calls, the 'tekiah', is an announcement of God's

Sovereignty. The watchman's duties include warning of impeding danger, aiding

preparations to combat those dangers, and announcing God's strategy and then His

Victory. These are vital answers to the question being asked in many quarters:

"Watchman, what of the night?"

This is of urgent importance as Europe and Russia stand on the cusp of nuclear

hostilities.

Chapter 13

A Burdensome Stone

The city of Jerusalem has herself been defined in Scripture as a stone, a particularly

difficult stone to deal with, a stone which causes injury, even a rupture to those who

try to move it, to those who try to tamper with the City's wellbeing and security.

"This is the word of the Lord concerning Israel. The Lord ... declares 'I will make

Jerusalem an immovable rock for all nations. All who try to move it will injure

themselves.'" (Zech.12:3)

The Crusaders' zealous motivation and stirring and flamboyant departures from

Europe, beginning in 1096 and onwards, were negated by the barbarism into which

they descended. They revelled in bloody massacres, both in the Holy City and

against Jewish communities along the route. The horrific sufferings the Crusaders

themselves endured, and the gruesome deaths they died, were more than matched by

the suffering they inflicted upon both Muslims and Jews.

The history of the Medieval quests, which wrested Jerusalem from Muslim control from 1099 to 1187 and again for fifteen years from 1229, distressingly exemplifies

the Biblical principle that Jerusalem becomes a cup of poison, a cup which sends

people reeling, to those who harm her (see Zec. 12:2).

In 1212 AD, many hundreds of Europe's children perished in the Children's

Crusade. During each of the other eight crusades the cream of Europe's young

manhood perished in battle, in shipwreck and in ambushes, while thousands more

died of infected wounds, smallpox and plague. When Saladin ousted the Crusaders

from Jerusalem they abandoned thousands of poor women, children and men. If they

could not afford to pay ransom money they were converted to Islam and became

slaves.

To their cost the British, among others, found Zechariah's warning to be true

between the two World Wars when they had a mandate to govern much of the Middle

East. It had suited their military purposes to take territory from Turkey, but they

found the land ungovernable: their conflicting national interests and loyalties to both

Jew and Arab were irreconcilable. The moral and financial cost of trying to carry the

stone became greater than they could bear and, so soon after World War II, the

British public was tired of warfare and the loss of life in the Middle East. Britain

handed the task of deciding on the future of the region over to the United Nations,

thus opening the way for the historic U.N. vote to be taken. On 29th November,

1947, the U.N. passed the resolution to create a sovereign state for Jewish refugees,

on the soil of their Ancient Homeland.

Israel is a stumbling block, a rock of offence, except to those whose intentions are

the same as God's intentions, whose actions are in line with Scripture. Thus we need

to ensure that our deeds and attitudes have the seal of Divine Favour upon them.

By contrast, many foreigners have helped Israel received the blessings promised in

Genesis 12:2, "I will bless those who bless you, and whoever curses you I will curse;

and all peoples on earth will be blessed through you." Examples include British

politicians Sir Winston Churchill and Lord Balfour, who both supported the

foundation of a Jewish homeland; General Edmund Allenby, to whom the keys of

Jerusalem were handed during World War I; Ord Wingate, whose military expertise

helped save the newly-born state; Conrad Schick, missionary, architect and

archaeologist, who helped found Christ Church Jaffa Gate and whose family home

still stands in the Street of the Prophets; Horatio and Anna Spafford, whose charity

work continues in the Old City; and Oscar Schindler, a 'righteous gentile', who is

buried just outside the Old City.

Chapter 14

How to Pray For Israel

1) Scripturally
   2) Thankfully
   3) Musically
   4) Joyfully
   5) Humbly
   6) Co-operatively
   7) Specifically
   8) Expectantly
   9) Persistently
   10) Unencumbered

1) SCRIPTURALLY

It is essential that watchmen, those who make mention of the Lord, who

acknowledge Him, must pray in harmony with God's purposes. This means that

prayer must be inspired by, and agree with, what the Scriptures reveal about the

Divine Intention. Daniel, an outstanding intercessor, has left us an example of this principle. Upon discovering the troubled state in which Jerusalem languished,

turning to the Lord he expressed his anguish, and petitioned the Lord's favour, with

fasting. Turning to the Scriptures, to the scroll of Jeremiah (Jer.29:10), he found the

promise that the exile in Babylon would last seventy years:

"I, Daniel, understood from the Scriptures, according to the word of the Lord given

to Jeremiah the prophet, that the desolation of Jerusalem would last seventy years."

(Dan. 9:2)

Daniel therefore knew how to pray in harmony with the will of God revealed in the

Scriptures and therefore was able to devote himself to Scripture-inspired

intercession. As a warrior of the Word he co-operated with God's eternal purposes.

He was far away from the walls of his beloved Jerusalem, yet he was her watchman.

"...I was speaking and praying, confessing my sin and the sin of my people Israel

and making my request to the Lord my God for his holy hill." (Dan.9:20)

Thus prayer for Israel must be based firmly on Scripture, on Scriptural context and

Scriptural principles, not on isolated verses and eccentric interpretations. When we

lay the Lord's own words before Him, in faith, we now that He will respond, and will honour His words and therefore our prayers. "The Lord said to me.... for I am

watching to see that my word is fulfilled." (Jer. 1:12)

2) THANKFULLY

The psalms abound with reasons for praise and gratitude; and with exhortations to

give thanks to the Lord. "Praise the Lord" (in Hebrew "Baruch Ha Shem") is used

throughout the Psalms, as an exhortation to thankfulness, and an affirmation of

gratitude. Psalms 136, 148, 149 and

150 list reasons why Israel should give thanks to the Lord - why praise should be

both their duty and the predominant attitude of their hearts.

We have even more reason for gratitude to the Lord than Ancient Israel, and we

cannot do less than they did. As Syria, Iran and Russia appear increasingly

threatening to Israel we must remember that it is scriptural to give thanks, rather than

dwelling anxiously on possible future threats.

"Extol the Lord, O Jerusalem; Praise your God, O Zion, for he strengthens the bars

of your gates and blesses your people within you. He grants peace to your borders

and satisfies you with the finest of wheat." (Ps. 147:12-14)

3) MUSICALLY

In Biblical Israel the joy of each of the regular festivals, of each special religious or royal celebration, and of each Sabbath worship experience, was enhanced by singing. Sabbath songs were unaccompanied, but congregational worship during

such magnificent occasions, just as the dedication of Solomon's Temple was

accompanied by large orchestras, grand choirs and much lively dancing.

There are many exhortations to praise God using musical instruments: woodwind,

strings, percussion and brass.

"Praise him with the sounding of the trumpet, praise him with the harp and lyre.

Praise him with tambourine and dancing, praise him with the strings and flute." (Ps.

150:3-4)

Dancing accompanied happy religious celebrations. Both priests and people were

involved but men and women danced separately.

"Let them praise his name with dancing..." (Ps. 149:3a) "Then maidens will dance

and be glad, young men and old as well". (Jer. 31:13a)

One family of dedicated gatekeepers, who were also musicians has left us a

praiseworthy example to follow. Jeduthun was a Levite, a descendant of Korah,

grandson of Kohath, son of Levi, and his family were 'keepers of the Temple

thresholds' just as their forefathers had been in the days of the Wilderness

Tabernacle.

"Heman and Jeduthun were responsible for the sounding of the trumpets and

cymbals and for the playing of the other instruments for sacred song. The sons of

Jeduthun were stationed at the gate." (1 Chron. 16:42)

Jeduthun's sons, under his supervision, were set apart for the multiple and powerful

ministries of intercession, of thanksgiving, of praise, worship, and of musically

accompanied prophesy - using harps, lyres and cymbals.

"David .. set apart some of the sons of Asaph, Heman and Jeduthun for the ministry

of prophesying, accompanied by harps, lyres and cymbals. Here is a list of men who

performed this service:... Jeduthun.. his sons, six in all, under the supervision of their

father Jeduthun, who prophesied, using the harp in thanking and praising the Lord."

(1 Chron. 25:1 & 3)

Of special note is one son, Obed-Edom, who became a doorkeeper for the Ark, and

keeper of the Temple treasures, (2 Chron. 25:24). He was appointed gatekeeper of

the South Gate, while his sons kept the

storehouse. Obed-Edom played the lyre and harp and ministered in music with his

eight sons and his sixty-two descendants.

"David told the leaders of the Levites to appoint their brothers as singers to sing

joyful songs, accompanied by musical instruments: lyres, harps and cymbals. So the

Levites appointed.... Obed-Edom and Jeiel, the gate-keepers." (1 Chron. 15:16-18)

Even Obed-Edom's grandsons were described as "very capable men.... leaders..

strong men, capable of doing the work (of the Lord)". Each man was chosen,

specifically designated by name, appointed to a ministry of praise - to give thanks to

the Lord for His goodness and the ministry of intercession was closely entwined with

whole-hearted praise.

"He (David) appointed some of the Levites to minister before the Ark of the Lord to

make petition, to give thanks, and to praise the Lord, the God of Israel: Asaph was

the chief, ... Obed-Edom and Jeiel. They were to play the lyres and harps." (1 Chron.

16:4 & 5b)

The Holy One had greatly blessed Obed-Edom, when, at David's request, he, for

three months, had cared for the Ark, symbol of the Presence, in his own home (see

2 Sam. 6:11).

Later, in the days of King Hezekiah, Jeduthun's family played a significant role in the purification of the newly finished Second Temple, (see 2 Chron. 29: 14-17). For

many generations this entire family exemplified the intimate connection between

willing service, purity of life, keeping of the gates, prayer, and ministering to the

Lord with music.

4) JOYFULLY

If music and dance are combined with a thankful heart, even if done simply in

obedience, without an emotional motivation, the inevitable outcome will be joy.

While thanksgiving is an act, a decision of the will, joy is a gift from God, a fruit of

the Spirit. While we cannot choose to have joy in the same way as we choose to

praise and to give thanks, we can anticipate that our praise will be rewarded and joy

will abound.

"Bring joy to your servant, for to you, O Lord, I lift up my soul." (Ps. 86:4)

5) HUMBLY

The people of Israel were required to bring their prayer requests before the Lord,

with the sacrifices of repentance and an awareness of the contrast between the Lord's

strength and righteousness and their own weakness and sin. These are the elements

of true humility.

Humility isn't slavish self-recrimination and obsequiousness, but real and truthful

self-evaluation, as Paul said: "not thinking of oneself more highly than we aught"

(Rom. 12:3). An acknowledgment of the Lord's righteous character and power will

prevent pride from impairing our prayers for Israel.

6) CO-OPERATIVELY

United prayer is effective prayer. Unity must be more than a physical gathering

together. The "upper room experience" was made possible

because the disciples prayed together physically, as well as with one accord, (see

Acts 1:14 & 2:1). Group prayer, if made in the presence of alternative agendas, is

thwarted.

"Can two walk together, except they be agreed?" (Amos 3:3 A.V.)

On the other hand unity of purpose and being of one heart and mind brings strength

and Divine favour.

"How good and pleasant it is when brothers live together in unity! For there the Lord

bestows his blessing, even life for evermore." (Ps. 133:1 & 3b)

7) SPECIFICALLY

As a warrior upon the ramparts does not fire his weapon aimlessly, or merely in the

general direction of the enemy, but selects his target, taking careful and specific aim,

so, also, the prayer warrior. Prayer is swifter than an arrow and precision is vital.

Specific prayers home in, onto the target, no matter what the subject matter.

"In everything, by prayer and petition, with thanksgiving, present your requests to

God." (Phil. 4:6b)

Here is one example of a very specific and detailed prayer request, shared, in unity,

by Paul and his prayer companions: "Night and day we pray most earnestly that we

may see you again and supply what is lacking in your faith. Now may our God and

Father himself and our Lord Jesus clear the way for us to come to you. May the Lord

make your love increase and overflow for each other and for everyone else, just as

ours does for you. May he strengthen your hearts so that you will be blameless and

holy in the presence of our God." (1 Thes. 3:10-13a)

8) EXPECTANTLY

The `prayer of faith' means that there is an expectation of an answer. This arises from

the knowledge that such prayer agrees with the Lord's will, as revealed in Scripture,

and is a Divinely appointed prayer-burden for this moment. The prayer which burns

in our hearts, which it is almost impossible NOT to pray, is, for us, a Spirit anointed

prayer.

"Therefore I tell you, whatever you ask for in prayer, believe that you have received

it, and it will be yours." (Mark 11:24)

9) PERSISTENTLY

The parables of the persistent widow who sought justice (Luke 18:5) and of the

friend who needed bread for his guests (Luke 11:5-10) teach us not to give up until

the answer is given. Consistent and continuous prayer, for each other, as well as for

Jerusalem, is so important:

"Since the day we heard about you, we have not stopped praying for you and

asking God to fill you with the knowledge of his will through all spiritual wisdom

and understanding." (Col. 1:9)

"I have posted watchmen on your walls, O Jerusalem; they will never be silent day

or night. You who call on the Lord, give your-selves no rest, and give him no rest

till he establish Jerusalem and make her the praise of the earth". (Is. 62:6-7)

10) UNENCUMBERED

The intercessor must be free of sins that so easily beset us and free from iniquity,

such as blasphemy, idolatry and pagan and occult influences.

"Let us throw off everything that hinders and the sin that so easily entangles, and

let us run with perseverance the race marked out for us. Let us fix our eyes on

Jesus." (Heb. 12:1b-2a)

Remember that Daniel confessed the sin of his people, as well as his own sin.

"...I was speaking and praying, confessing my sin and the sin of my people Israel

and making my request to the Lord my God for his holy hill." (Dan.9:20)

Moses was another great leader who stood in the gap for the Hebrew people after

they had worshiped the golden calf so that God intended to destroy them,

"- had not Moses his chosen one, stood in the breach before Him and kept His

wrath from destroying them." (Ps. 106:23).

The Christian must also not be encumbered with hidden sins like resentment, anger

and un-forgiveness. As Jesus taught, forgiveness is essential, not just God's

forgiveness of us, but also our forgiveness of one another. Un-forgiveness is a

heavy load to carry and an impediment to spiritual victory.

"Be kind and compassionate to one another, forgiving each other, just as in Christ
God forgave you." (Eph. 4:32)

Chapter 15

For My Brothers' Sake

We know that many of the world's watchmen have been faithful in prayer, because

we see that the promises of the Bible are currently being fulfilled. Of particular

note are the promises to regather the Jewish people, and to settle them in the Land

of Israel with His blessing, promises such as these:

"'The days are coming' declares the Lord, 'when I will bring my people Israel and

Judah back from captivity and restore them to the land I gave to their forefathers

to possess.'" (Jer. 30:3)

" See, I will bring them from the land of the north and gather them from the ends of

the earth." (Jer. 31:8a)

As yet fewer than half of the world's fourteen million identified Jews live in Israel.

The majority remain in the U.S.A.: but every day hundreds stream back from

Russia (the land of the north), and from Africa, far away Argentina, and the ends

of the earth. This is a direct fulfilment of prophesy found throughout the

Scriptures; and the fact that it is coming to pass while these words are being read,

bears testimony to the faithfulness of those who, in the
past, were called to be
prayer-watchmen for Israel.

Will this generation be as faithful?

Or does it seem that the task is finished, or that the current
Exodus has its own
momentum and will thus automatically be completed?

The truth is that the easy part is behind, and the difficult
part still ahead. For example
it is the well-educated and well-informed who have come
out of Eastern Europe so
far. Generally they are from the major and more easily
accessible cities. Conversely
those who are less prosperous, less resilient, less
adventurous, less convinced, less
able to travel, and more isolated, will be much harder to
rescue; yet they are the more
vulnerable, and anti-Semitism is gaining strength. The rise
of ultra-nationalist and
Neo-Nazi movements in the former communist block;
political, moral and economic
instability in Eastern Europe and the terrible war in
Ukraine should convince us all
that the intercessor's task is by no means over.

There are other aspects of the Divine purpose for Israel
which need to be enveloped
in prayer until they come to pass. Of specific current
importance is the injunction to
pray for Israel's prosperity in these days of global inflation
and threatened recession,

to pray for the strength and stability of her economy, and for her peace: not just a temporary man-made peace, but Shalom from On High. Pray for the promised peace;

the gift of the Prince of Peace:

"May there be peace within thy walls and prosperity within thy palaces." (Ps. 122:7

A.V.)

All of the as yet unfulfilled prophesies of the Scriptures are pertinent to Israel. Every

year it becomes more obvious that Israel is the crucible of the world and the centre

of the Divine agenda. This Land should therefore be at the centre of our devoted

intercessions. It is imperative that prayer for Israel should be our urgent and faithful

business, and also our great privilege.

Any who believe that they do not have a calling to pray for Israel will miss the

opportunity of praying in harmony with God's final purposes for the Earth and its

people, of praying for all of His good purposes:

"For I will create Jerusalem to be a delight and its people a joy. I will rejoice over

Jerusalem and take delight in my people." (Is. 65:18-19)

The truth is that continuous and heart-felt prayer is to be offered for Israel "until" ..

Until when? Until the Lord responds, and answers in harmony with His promises

to Israel. Let us, like Isaiah, make this promise:

"For Zion's sake I will not keep silent, for Jerusalem's sake I will not rest, until her

vindication goes forth as brightness, and her salvation as a burning torch." (Is.
62:1 RSV)
Israel
the day of your watchmen has come!!

Plate 15.1. Timeless prayer at the Western Wall. Public domain.

"Her stones are dear to your servants. Her very dust moves them
to pity." (Ps. 102:14)

Books by Dr Deslee Campbell

<u>Synagogue and Church Series (Bible and Archaeology)</u>:
   Synagogues of 'the Jesus Period'
   Family, Society and Cultural Life in Galilee
   The Other Holy Lands: Egypt, Jordan, Syria and Lebanon
   Jerusalem of Gold (second edition)
   Ancient Ephesus and Earliest Christianity
   Why a Roman Emperor Rebuilt Jerusalem and Jerash
   The Olive Tree: an exposition of Romans 9-11
   Stones, Walls and Watchmen (second edition)
   Pilgrimage to Israel and Jordan

<u>'Shoah' Educational Series</u>:

Voices From The Silence
   Confronting Holocaust Denial

<u>Biographies of Memorable People</u>:

Phoebe's Sisters: Women Leaders in Early Christianity
   Bright Shining Lights of an Earlier Era
   Shining Lights of the Reformation
   Remarkable Christians of the Post-Reformation Era
   Modern Christian Martyrs
   Great Christian Men We Have Forgotten
   Great Christian Women We Have Forgotten

Christian Women Leaders of the 20th Century

Mothers in Israel

Novels:

Kaleidoscope of Life
Love is a Journey
The Topkapi Beggar

Books Co-Authored with Rev. Justin Campbell:

Synagoga's Heritage: Tabernacle, Temple, Synagogue and Church
Ecclesia: The Long Journey to Tomorrow
Grow Your Church: THE Challenge of the 21st Century

Also by Deslee Campbell

The Topkapi Beggar
Voices From The Silence
Why a Roman Emperor Rebuilt Jerusalem and Jerash
Stones, Walls and Watchmen
Mothers in Israel

Watch for more at www.synagogueandchurch.com.

About the Author

Deslee Campbell, a former teacher of modern history, who worked in the field of educational psychology andcounselling.She has a Bachelor of Arts degree from the University of New South Wales, a Diploma in Education from the University of Sydney, and a Graduate Diploma in School Counselling from U.W.S/Nepean.She was has a Masters degree fromMacquarie University in early Christian Studies and a Phd from Sydney University.Deslee has visited Israel nine times, the first being in January 1970. During Passover 1990 Deslee was one of threeAustralians to visit the U.S.S.R. Since 1988 Deslee, and her late husband John, .they lived with their three sons and their adopted daughter in Sydney and attend a local Anglican Church in Sydney, Now widowed, Deslee has four children and three grandchildren.Her published works include the sequel novel, Love is a Journey, which follows Karen Evan's career as a nurse.With her son, Rev. Justin Campbell, she has co-authored a major 2-volume work in the mini-series Synagogue andChurch and her YouTube presentations can be viewed via the web addresshttp://www.synagogueandchurch.com

Read more at www.synagogueandchurch.com.

www.ingramcontent.com/pod-product-compliance
Lightning Source LLC
Chambersburg PA
CBHW071951150726

47999CB00001B/405